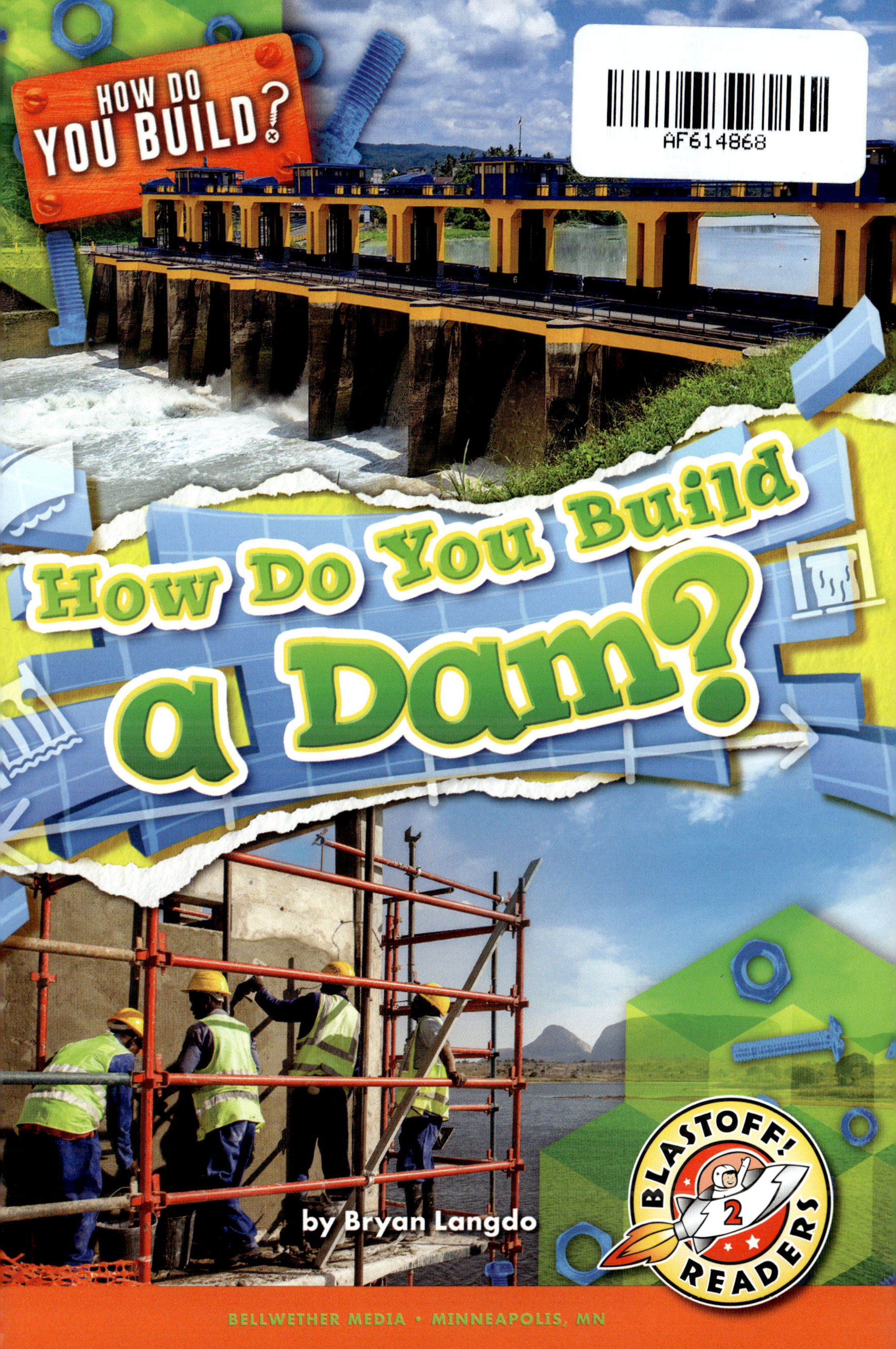

How Do You Build a Dam?

by Bryan Langdo

BELLWETHER MEDIA • MINNEAPOLIS, MN

Blastoff! Readers are carefully developed by literacy experts to build reading stamina and move students toward fluency by combining standards-based content with developmentally appropriate text.

Level 1 provides the most support through repetition of high-frequency words, light text, predictable sentence patterns, and strong visual support.

Level 2 offers early readers a bit more challenge through varied sentences, increased text load, and text-supportive special features.

Level 3 advances early-fluent readers toward fluency through increased text load, less reliance on photos, advancing concepts, longer sentences, and more complex special features.

★ **Blastoff! Universe**

Reading Level

Grade K

Grades 1–3

Grade 4

This edition first published in 2026 by Bellwether Media, Inc.

Library of Congress Cataloging-in-Publication Data

LC record for How Do You Build a Dam? available at: https://lccn.loc.gov/2025010700

Editor: Rachael Barnes Book Designer: Josh Brink

Printed in the United States of America, North Mankato, MN.

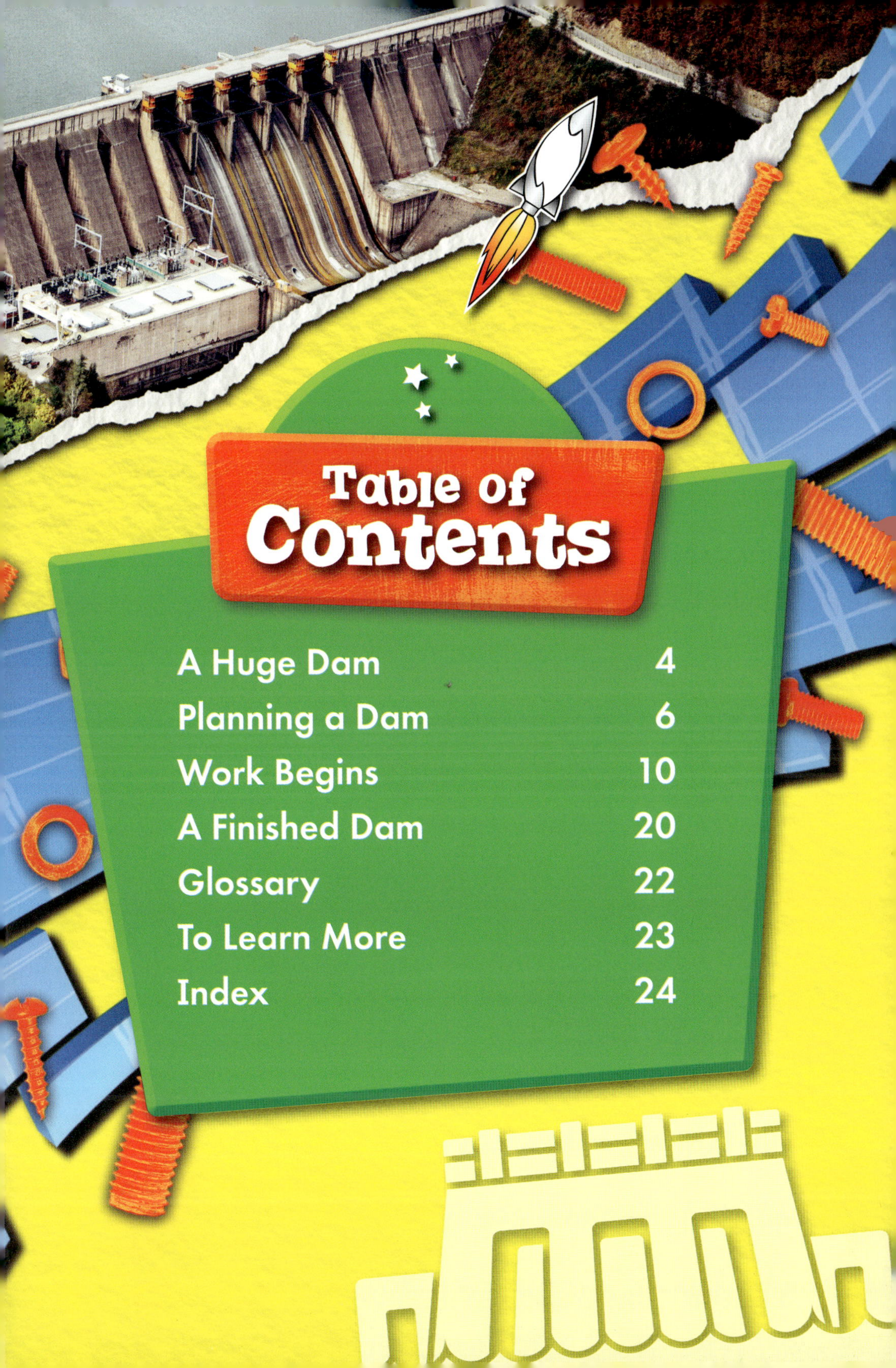

Table of Contents

A Huge Dam 4
Planning a Dam 6
Work Begins 10
A Finished Dam 20
Glossary 22
To Learn More 23
Index 24

A Huge Dam

Boats float down a river.
A blue heron hunts fish.

A huge wall rises above the river. It is a dam!

Planning a Dam

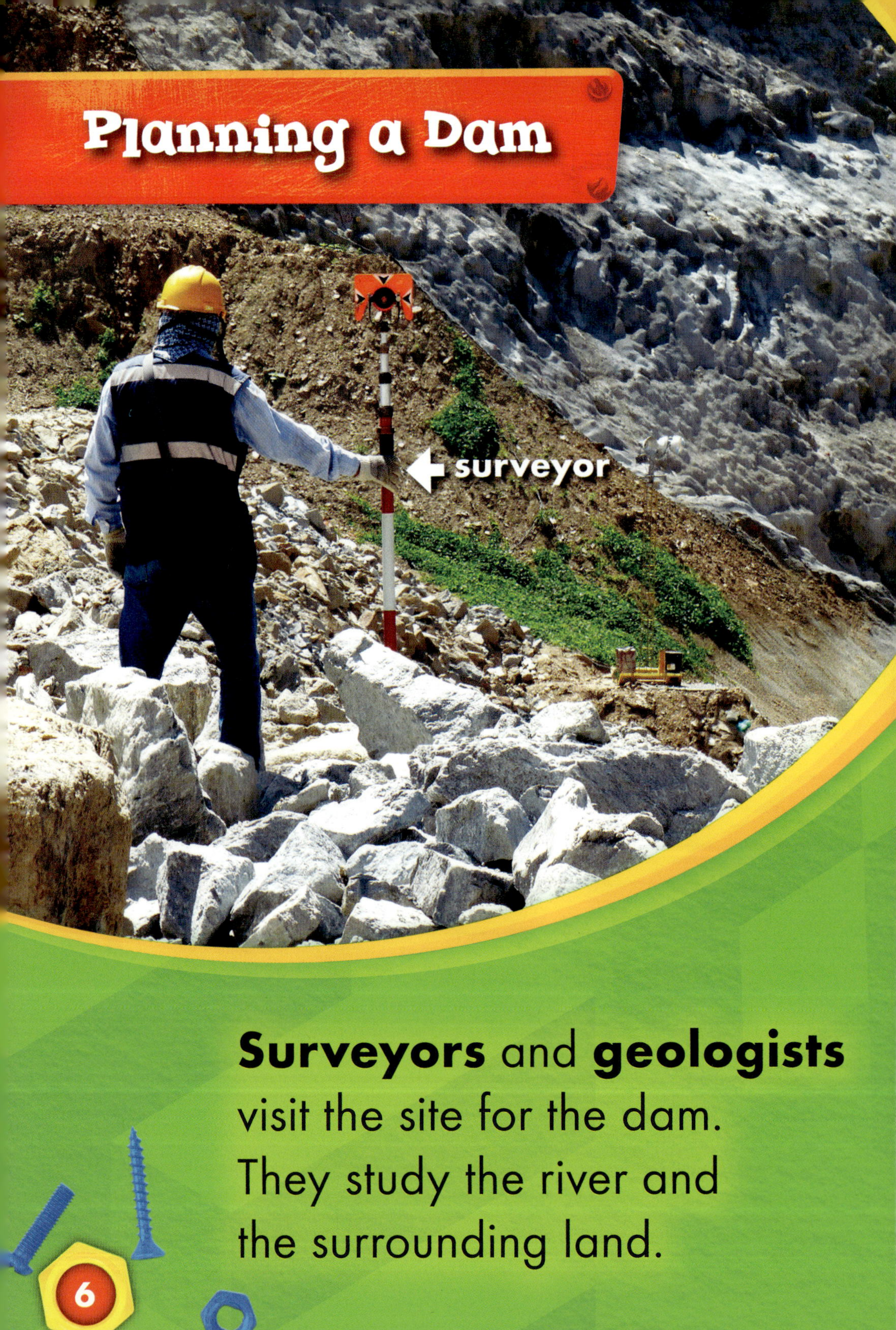

Surveyors and **geologists** visit the site for the dam. They study the river and the surrounding land.

Engineers use what they learn about the site to **design** the dam.

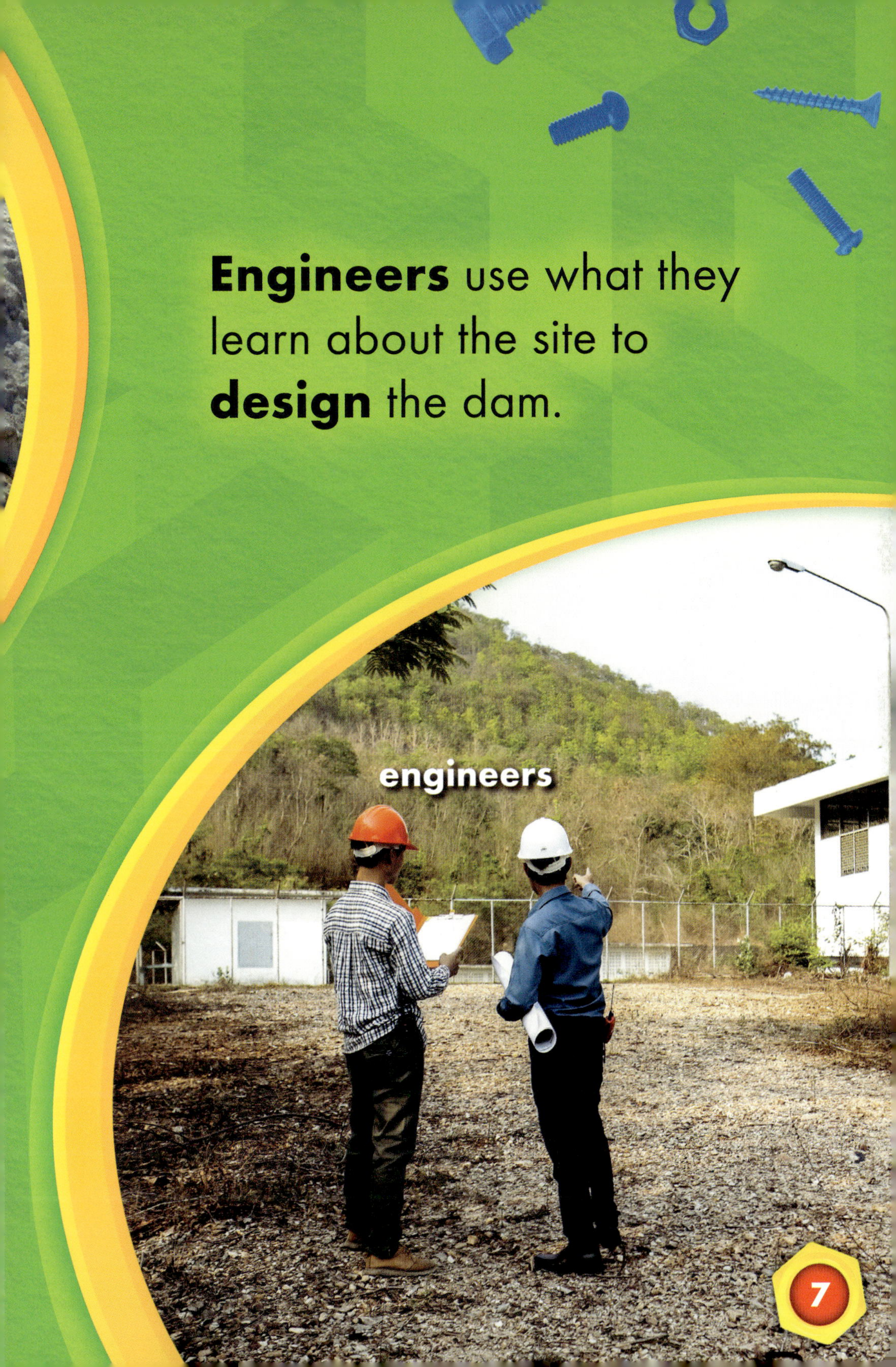

Workers must redirect the river. They often dig **diversion channels**.

This makes part of the **riverbed** dry. Work can begin!

Work Begins

The dam's **foundation** is built first. Machines remove loose soil.

Rocks and **grout** are used to fill in any cracks.

 What Do You Need? 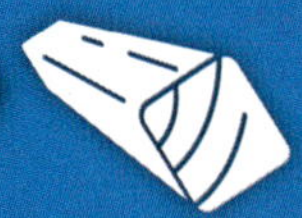

rocks

wood

concrete

steel

concrete

steel bars

Workers build wood frames with steel bars inside. They pour **concrete** into the frames.

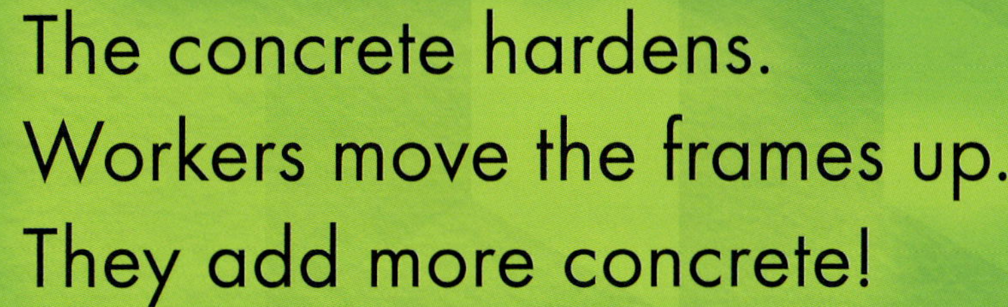

The concrete hardens.
Workers move the frames up.
They add more concrete!

Parts of a Dam

reservoir
crest
spillway
foundation

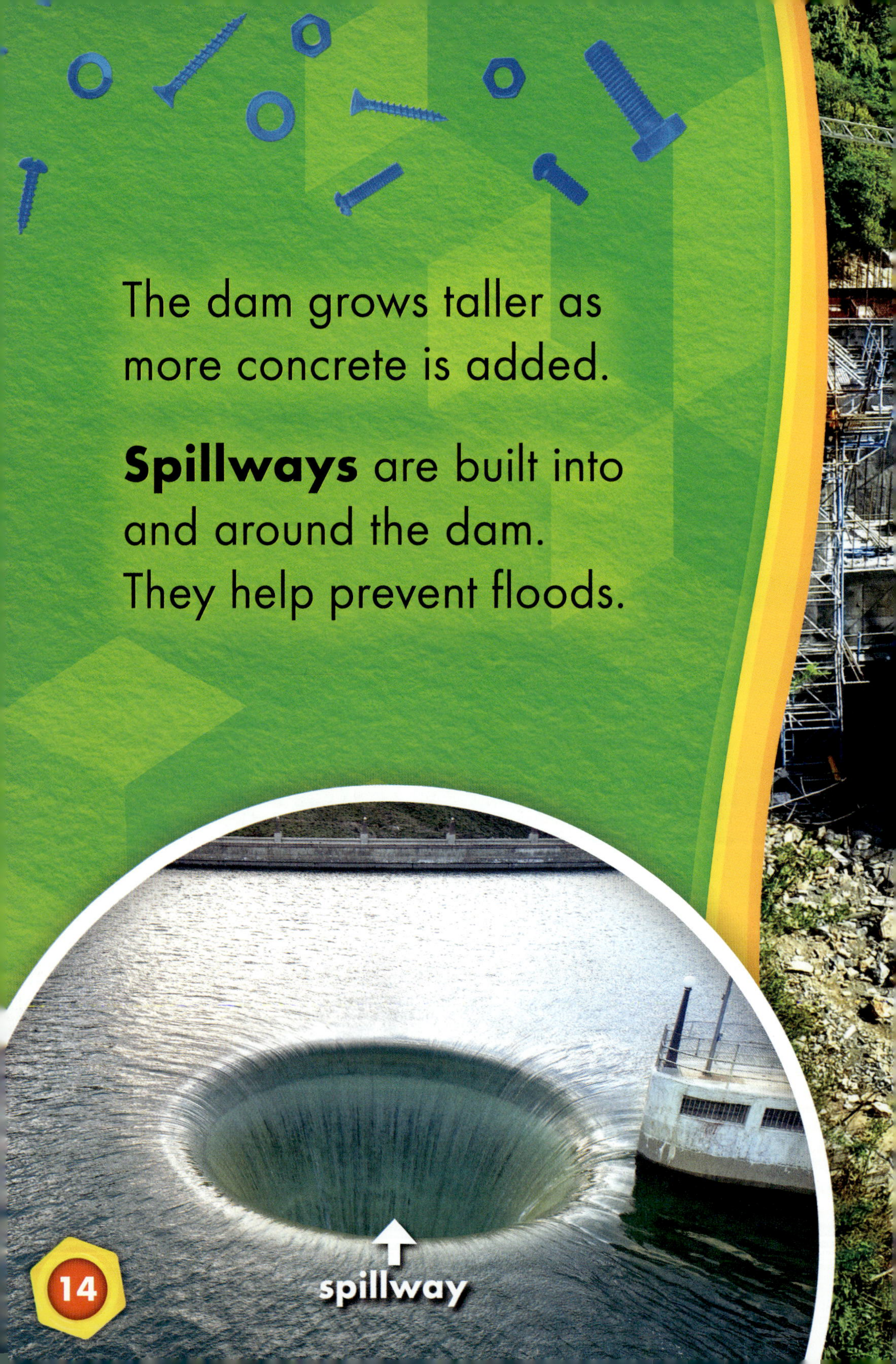

The dam grows taller as more concrete is added.

Spillways are built into and around the dam. They help prevent floods.

spillway

The final layer of concrete forms the top of the dam. It is called the crest.

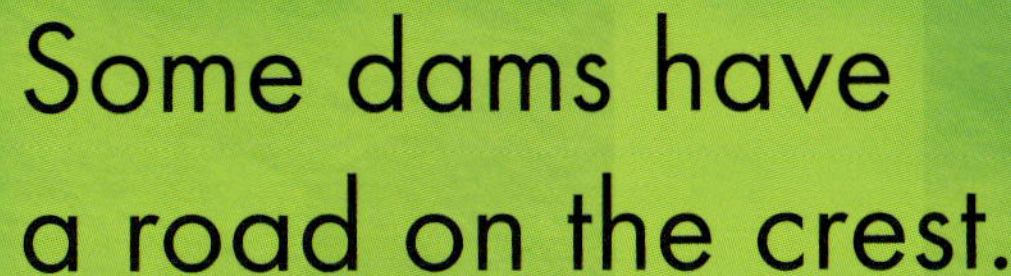

Some dams have a road on the crest.

Jinping-I Dam

Location Sichuan, China

Height 1,001 feet (305 meters)

Year completed 2012

Famous for the tallest dam in the world

inspectors

Diversion channels are removed. Water slowly rises behind the dam. **Inspectors** check for leaks.

1. Workers study the site and design the dam.

2. The river is redirected.

4. Workers pour concrete into frames.

5. A reservoir forms behind the dam.

6. Inspectors check the dam for leaks.

The water forms a **reservoir**. Some reservoirs take years to fill!

A Finished Dam

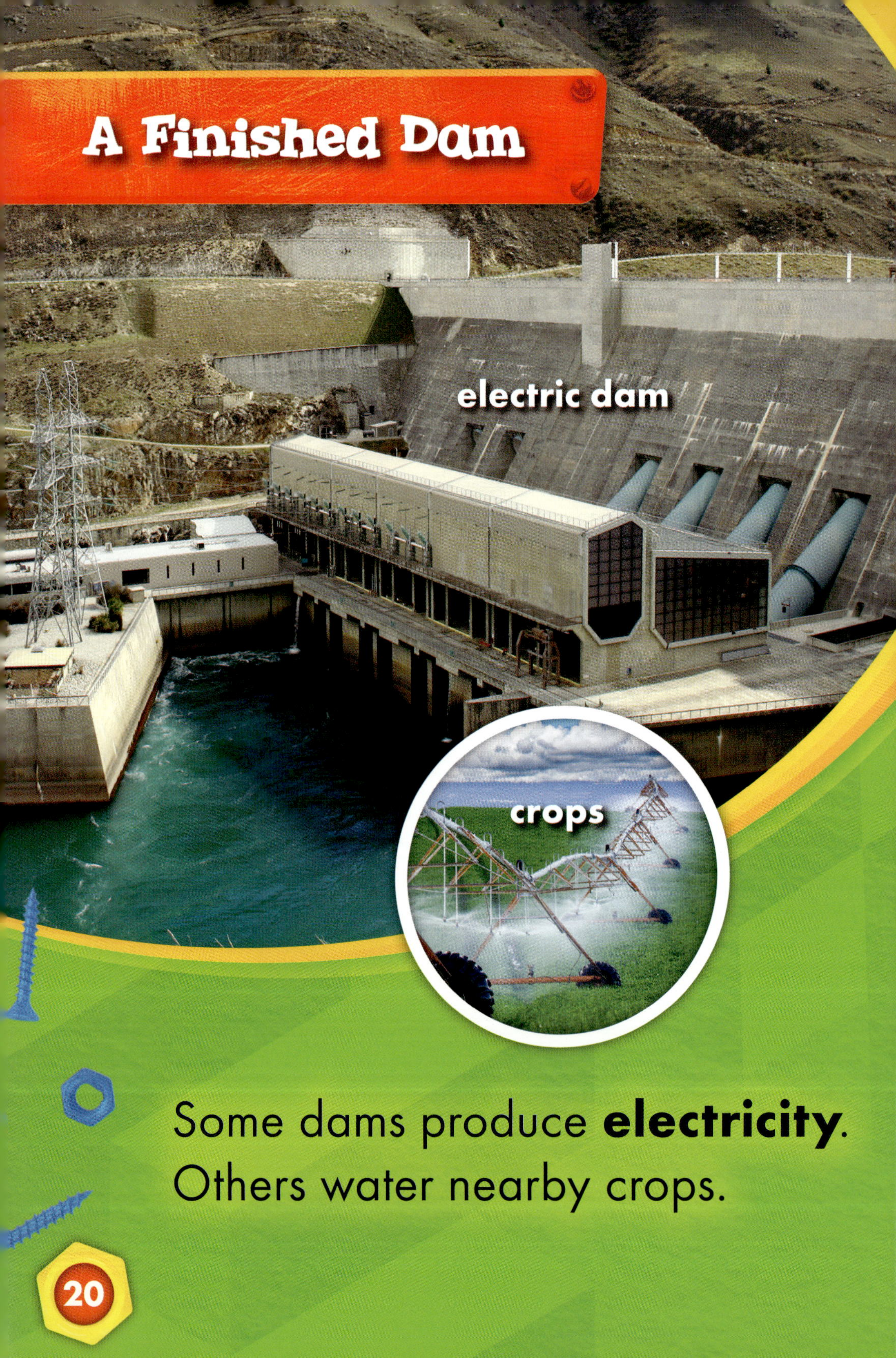

Some dams produce **electricity**. Others water nearby crops.

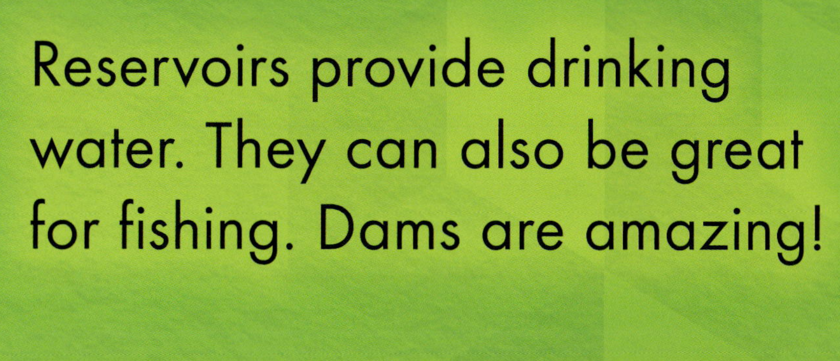

Reservoirs provide drinking water. They can also be great for fishing. Dams are amazing!

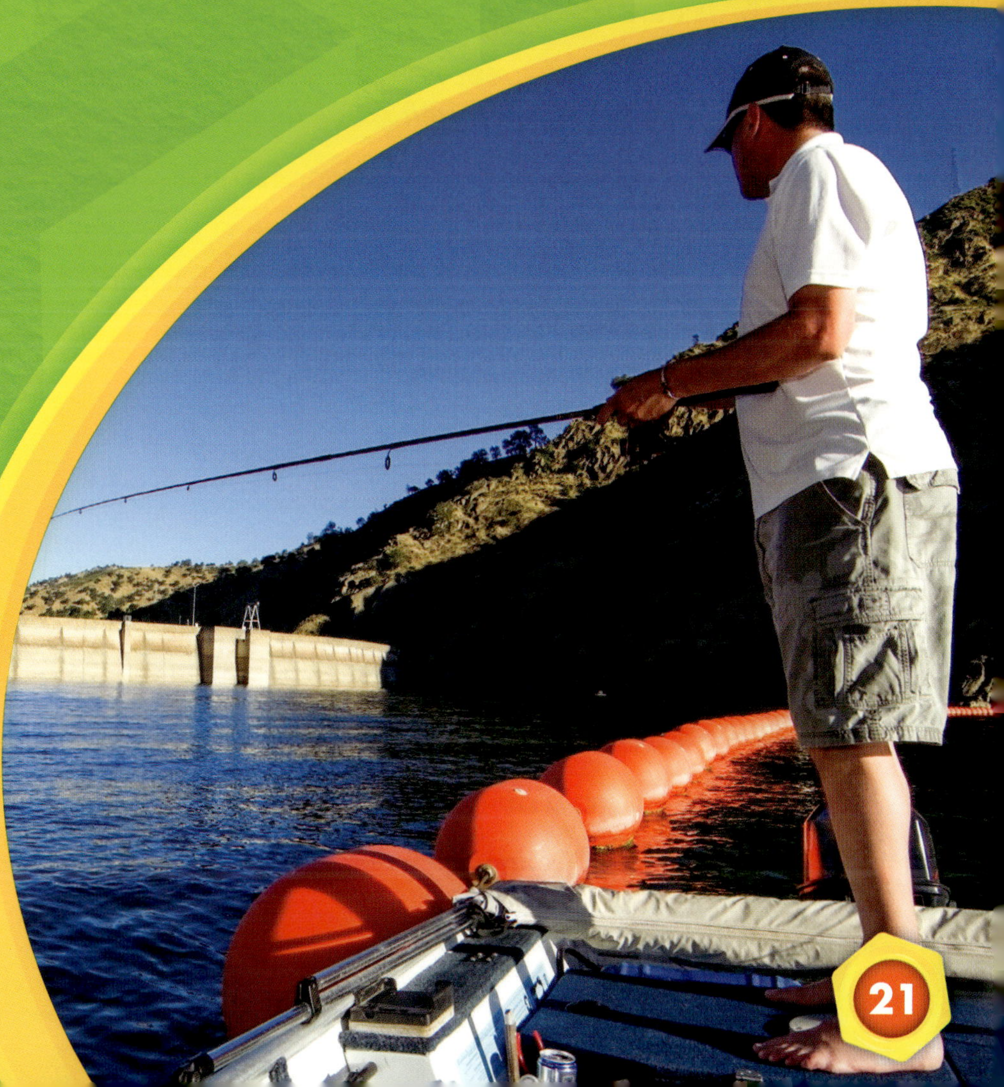

Glossary

concrete—a hard, strong building material made with cement, sand, rocks, and water

design—to make a plan for building a dam or other structure

diversion channels—human-made paths that make a river flow somewhere else temporarily

electricity—power that is carried through wires and is used to run machines

engineers—people who are trained to design and build machines, systems, or structures

foundation—a base or support on top of which a structure is built

geologists—scientists who study what Earth is made of

grout—a mixture of sand, water, and cement used to fill spaces

inspectors—people who check to make sure work was done correctly

reservoir—a human-made lake made to store water

riverbed—the soil and rock that forms the bottom of a river

spillways—passages that let extra water flow over or around a dam

surveyors—people who measure areas of land for different projects

To Learn More

AT THE LIBRARY

Dittmer, Lori. *Hoover Dam.* Mankato, Minn.: Creative Education/Creative Paperbacks, 2020.

Fehr, Daniel. *Let's Build a Dam!* New York, N.Y.: NorthSouth Books, 2023.

Kenney, Karen Latchana. *Energy from Moving Water.* Minneapolis, Minn.: Bearport, 2022.

ON THE WEB

FACTSURFER

Factsurfer.com gives you a safe, fun way to find more information.

1. Go to www.factsurfer.com.
2. Enter "dam" into the search box and click 🔍.
3. Select your book cover to see a list of related content.

Index

concrete, 12, 13, 14, 16
crest, 16, 17
crops, 20
design, 7
diversion channels, 8, 18
electricity, 20
engineers, 7
fishing, 21
foundation, 10
frames, 12, 13
geologists, 6
grout, 10, 11
inspectors, 18
Jinping-I Dam, 17
parts of a dam, 13
reservoir, 19, 21
river, 4, 6, 8, 9
road, 16, 17
rocks, 11
site, 6, 7
spillways, 14
steel bars, 12
step by step, 19
surveyors, 6
water, 18, 19, 20, 21
what do you need?, 11
workers, 8, 12, 13

The images in this book are reproduced through the courtesy of: Andi baso amry, cover (top hero); Jake Lyell/ Alamy, cover (bottom hero); zorandim75, pp. 2-3 (dam); John L. Absher, p. 4; AlexPapp, pp. 4-5; Ricardo Vallejo Vieira, p. 6; KoOlyphoto, p. 7; marekuliasz, p. 8; Washington State Dept of Transportation, p. 8 (inset photo); Alexey Slyusarenko, p. 9; bannafarsai, p. 10; Sumith Nunkham, p. 10 (grout); aleks1313, p. 11 (rocks); shablovskyistock, p. 11 (wood); Shine Nucha, p. 11 (concrete); Guiderom, p. 11 (steel); oneSHUTTER oneMEMORY, p. 12; PRANEE JIRAKITDACHAKUN, p. 12 (inset photo); Autumn Sky, p. 13; txking, p. 14; orin, pp. 14-15; Olha Solodenko, p. 16; Bryan Busovicki, p. 16 (road); Imaginechina/ Alamy, p. 17; APFootage/ Alamy, pp. 18-19; Operation 2022/ Alamy, p. 19 (step one); Markus Volk, p. 19 (step two); Polbkt, p. 19 (step three); guvendemir, p. 19 (step four); CLI/ Wikipedia, p. 19 (step five); Matthias Bein/ AP Images, p. 19 (step six); ocwo, p. 20; Bob Pool, p. 20 (inset photo); Michael Ireland, p. 21; Patrick Ziegler, pp. 22-23, 24 (background); NaMo Stock, p. 23.